ISBN 978-1-330-64808-7
PIBN 10087175

This book is a reproduction of an important historical work. Forgotten Books uses state-of-the-art technology to digitally reconstruct the work, preserving the original format whilst repairing imperfections present in the aged copy. In rare cases, an imperfection in the original, such as a blemish or missing page, may be replicated in our edition. We do, however, repair the vast majority of imperfections successfully; any imperfections that remain are intentionally left to preserve the state of such historical works.

1 MONTH OF
FREE
READING

at

www.ForgottenBooks.com

By purchasing this book you are eligible for one month membership to ForgottenBooks.com, giving you unlimited access to our entire collection of over 700,000 titles via our web site and mobile apps.

To claim your free month visit:

www.forgottenbooks.com/free87175

English
Français
Deutsche
Italiano
Español
Português

www.forgottenbooks.com

Mythology Photography **Fiction**
Fishing Christianity **Art** Cooking
Essays Buddhism Freemasonry
Medicine **Biology** Music **Ancient**
Egypt Evolution Carpentry Physics
Dance Geology **Mathematics** Fitness
Shakespeare **Folklore** Yoga Marketing
Confidence Immortality Biographies
Poetry **Psychology** Witchcraft
Electronics Chemistry History **Law**
Accounting **Philosophy** Anthropology
Alchemy Drama Quantum Mechanics
Atheism Sexual Health **Ancient History**
Entrepreneurship Languages Sport
Paleontology Needlework Islam
Metaphysics Investment Archaeology
Parenting Statistics Criminology
Motivational

UCLA

UNIVERSITY RESEARCH LIBRARY

Department of Special Collections

 споо

EXHIBITION CATALOGUE

PHILODEMUS AND GREEK PAPYRI

by

PAUL G. NAIDITCH
REBECCA RESINSKI

U C L A

UNIVERSITY RESEARCH LIBRARY

Department of Special Collections

☙

EXHIBITION CATALOGUE

An exhibition

1 April - 31 August 199

Department of Special Collections
University Research Library
University of California
Los Angeles

philodemus

and

greek papy

by

Paul G. Naiditch
Rebecca Resinski

Title-page design by Sue A. Kaplan
Department of Special Collections, UCLA
The background is P.Herc. 207

* * *

This Catalogue is produced with support from
The Bernadine J. L. M. Zelenka Endowment

THE DEVELOPMENT OF PAPYROLOGY

by

Paul G. Naiditch

Coming to the island of Chios in the year 1749, the Irish traveller Lord Charlemont observed that its Monastery possessed "a sort of library with many manuscripts lying in dust and rubbish. We spent an hour looking them over, hoping to have discovered some ancient treasure, but found nothing but some manuscripts of the Greek Fathers".[1] Charlemont's desire to locate notable classical works was hardly limited to him: it belonged to an old tradition.

Efforts to recover manuscripts of classical writings reach back to antiquity itself. These were, inevitably, both occasional in nature as well as rigorous and deliberate. Only a few attempts, however, were systematic. Perhaps most notable were the efforts made at the Library of Alexandria. Over twenty-two hundred years ago, its collections contained hundreds of thousands of papyrus rolls. These survived at least for two centuries and not impossibly for half a millennium or more. Eventually, however, they were lost. The rolls themselves, whether burnt by Caesar's fire or destroyed by disintegration, infestation, accident, censorship, or indifference, disappeared. Additional copies, if they were produced, were insufficient to preserve the collections; and, with the decline of interest in classical literature, there was in addition less incentive either to copy texts anew or to preserve texts already in existence. During the second century of the common era, the works of scores of authors had been available: by the fifth century, it appears that only a handful of authors were regularly read or consulted; and much of classical literature was lost.

In the fourteenth century and the fifteenth another notable attempt to recover the classics was inaugurated. Inspired by Petrarch and his circle, enthusiasts undertook to retrieve and revivify the literature of classical antiquity. Petrarch himself has been described as "the first man since antiquity to make a systematic collection of Latin classical manuscripts".[2] His friends and successors continued his work, and the invention of printing established on a firm basis, and made generally available, the texts thus laboriously or fortuitously recovered.[3] Indeed, most of the ancient compositions included in classical series today were first printed in the fifteenth or sixteenth century: Latin classics notably by the printers Sweynheym and Pannartz, Johann de Spira, and Nicolaus Jenson, the Greek classics chiefly by Aldus Manutius and his heirs, Froben and the Stephani.

The discovery of classical writings did not cease with the 1500's. Yet, after mid-century, those new works that came to light were of less interest to the majority of scholars and men of letters than those that earlier had been found. Where previous years had seen the first published editions of major works, writings by Cicero, Vergil, and Livy, Homer, Aristotle, Thucydides, Sophocles, Aeschylus, and Pindar, the latter had to be content with Appian, Aretaeus, Aristaenetus and Antoninus Liberalis: authors not without significance, but also unlikely to excite general interest or enthusiasm. Later still, editiones principes of works such as Manetho's astrological poem, the *Apotelesmatica* (first printed, 1698), perhaps understandably failed to delight even the majority of classical scholars.[4]

But hope that heretofore unexplored libraries, especially those under Turkish control in Greece, Constantinople, the Holy Land and Egypt, would reveal lost works of classical antiquity never failed. It was, however, a hope that was often ill-founded. Yet when the first new roadway leading to a rediscovery of the classics was found, circumstances prevented its appreciation; and this failure of imagination delayed the development of papyrology for nearly a century and a half.

*   *   *

Whilst Lord Charlemont was visiting Greece and Turkey in search of classical manuscripts, and commenting adversely both on the contents of libraries and on the conditions he found an anonymous satirist was, at almost exactly the same time, inadvertently prophesying the future. Pretending that manuscripts had been discovered at Herculaneum, the satirist wrote:

> When I have given you an account, from time to time, of the discoveries that have been made in the the the city of Herculaneum, you have thanked me indeed, but you have always seemed dissatisfied at their not meeting with any one book, among all the various curiosities which have been found there. I have longed much to satisfy you; and have with you wondered much, that nothing of that kind should have appeared: for a city of people that never read, in so polite a part of the world too, as this was in Pliny's time (when the city, it seems, was overwhelmed) would be a very strange thing; and not a little disgraceful to the inhabitants. But the character of the Herculanenses is now likely to be cleared of that ignominy: for we have at length met with an evidence, that some of them probably did read; and that not only in their own language, but in such strange ones, as nobody now living can make any thing of.[5]

Only a few years afterwards, in 1752-1754, a classical library was found at Herculaneum: the first classical library ever to come to light, and even now the largest ever discovered.[6]

Herculaneum, one of the cities overwhelmed by the eruption of Vesuvius in 79 C.E., was discovered by chance towards the beginning of the eighteenth century. In digging a well, fragments of marble were found. Prince d'Elboeuf, learning of this, arranged for more marble to be sought for his pleasure dome: instead of mere marble, sculptures revealed themselves. Later Carlo III, King of the Two Sicilies, apparently at the instance of his wife Maria Amalia, arranged for excavations to be renewed. Archaeology as a science was not yet in existence, and these excavations were anything but scientific: holes were bored, art was removed. The discovery of classical manuscripts was only one of many discoveries.

The papyri found at Herculaneum were not instantly recognised as books. In part this was due to their physical condition, for they seemed little more than carbonised lumps. In addition, relatively few fully appreciated the idea that the Greeks and Romans used papyrus as paper. Of course, the elder Pliny had described papyrus in his encyclopedia. This encyclopedia had been printed as early as 1469; it was often reissued and, despite its great length, not infrequently translated into European languages. And experts in palaeography, such as Montfaucon, were alive to the nature of papyrus.[7] But probably most men of letters of the period had never seen papyrus, and did not really realise that it was once in common use. The anonymous British satirist, for example, describes his "Herculanean" manuscripts as having been written "on a sort of paper, made of the bark of trees".[8]

The discovery at Herculaneum was widely publicised, though at first inaccurately. "Upwards of one hundred rolls of Greek manuscripts, on vellum, most of them very legible, have at length been found in the ruins of Herculaneum. His Sicilian Majesty has appointed a committee of the most learned men in his dominions to examine them; and great hopes are entertained, that there are among them some works of the ancients which have long been lost to the learned world".[9] Reports soon became common: in Great Britain, one comes on accounts in the *Gentleman's Magazine*, in the *Critical Review*, in the *Monthly Review*, in the *Universal Magazine*, in the *London Magazine*, and especially in the *Philosophical Transactions*.[10] Not long after the discovery was announced, in 1755, M. de la Condamine toured Italy, and called the new manuscripts the "most valuable" material recovered from the excavations.[11]

> The most valuable beyond doubt of all the monuments which are admired there, is the great number of manuscripts on Egyptian paper, blackened and almost calcined, and nearly in the same state as if drawn out of an oven. They have found out, however, the art of unrolling them, and of gluing the leaves on a very thin pellicle; happily they are written but on one side. They are now labouring to transcribe these manuscripts, which it requires only time to do: They will, no doubt, hereafter succeed so far as to interpret them; they are all Greek. The characters of those I have seen are very distinct; I have read, without difficulty, many words in them, and even entire lines.

These manuscripts fostered hopes that lost classical writings would be recovered. One comes on the opinion again and again: e.g.,

> je veux dire, sur une maison écartée, consacrée aux muses, dans laquelle on eût trouvé complets qui nous manquent toujours, comme un Diodore de Sicile, un Polybe, un Saluste, un Tite Live, un Tacite [sic], la seconde parte des fastes d'Ovide, les vingt-quatre livres de la guerre des Germains, que Pline commença lorsqu'il servoit dans ce pays; ou bien enfin, puisque ce peuple aimoit tant le théâtre, un Eschyle, un Eurypide, un Aristophane, un Ménandre; certes on pouvoit se flatter de ce dernier genre de découvertes.[12]

In the event, the library was devoted to Epicurean philosophy, with which the eighteenth century had little sympathy, and much of the collection consisted of copies of Philodemus.

Where readers expected major poets, dramatists and historians, a philosopher such as Philodemus was a disappointment. Scarcely a year passed before a reporter affirmed: "It is assured, that such fragments of manuscripts as have been found in the ruins of Herculaneum, and have with great difficulty been rendered legible, prove to be no more than sentences out of Epicurean philosophers, who would persuade their readers, that as the world was made and subsists by chance, they are at liberty to live at random". Then, too, Sir William Gell judged that "The time and assiduous caution required, renders the unrolling them a work of tedious difficulty, not hitherto rewarded by the discovery of any work of consequence; though the learned world must ever feel grateful to the munificence of the Regent". Finally, in a review of 1847, it was said: "If Omar, according to the tale, burned the library of Alexandria, we have doubts whether he ought not to be honoured as a benefactor of our race. The fragments of works found in Herculaneum, – the manuscripts discovered in the Greek monasteries, Turkey, and a very large proportion of the palimpsests so laboriously deciphered, have given us scarcely anything that is either of interest or value. There has been little disinterred within the last half century which merited the honours of a resurrection".[13]

It was disappointment, too, that led Thomas Gaisford to write: "I am much more sanguine as to the good to be derived from the Farnese & other MSS in the royal and conventual libraries in that city (Naples) than that which some people think likely to arise from the unrolling of the Herculaneum cinders".[14] Gaisford had been impressed by recent discoveries in Italy and by Sir Humphry Davy's formal report on the Herculanean papyri. In Italy, Angelo Mai was examining palimpsests with care and finding, for instance, lost orations and letters of Fronto, fragments of lost speeches by Cicero, and a late antique text of Plautus containing a text superior to all others. So also, in this period, Aucber uncovered the Armenian version of Eusebius's *Chronicle*: a work then known only from extracts and Jerome's translation of one book. And, at length, Mai found palimpsests containing large portions of Cicero's *De Republica*. Meanwhile Davy, examining the papyri, had reached the dismal conclusion that no more than 80-120 of the remaining Herculanean papyri would repay examination.[15]

Other papyri discoveries proved inadequate to outweigh the disappointment in the Herculanean rolls. In 1788, the first papyrus roll from Egypt was edited by Nicolaus Schow, who wrote:

> The papyrus roll of the Museum Borgianum was discovered, together with forty or fifty others, in the year 1778 in a certain underground location of the city of Giza, in which region, as is known, ancient Memphis was commonly believed to be situated. All of these papyri (I do not know in what manner they were rolled), having been stored in a kind of chest made of cedar wood, were offered to a merchant at some slight cost. He, ignorant however of the value and worth of these works, purchased only one (which is ours) on account of its novelty, and had it sent to the most great secretary Stefano Borgia: the rest, the Turks tore apart, and rejoiced themselves in their fumes (for they say that the fumes were aromatic).[16]

The single document Schow published appears to have excited little interest. So also other papyri finds, though better publicised, likewise did not attract much regard. In 1847, for example, James Harris announced to the Royal Society of Literature in London that he had acquired a papyrus of Hyperides, an Attic orator of the fourth century B.C.E., whose speeches had long been desiderated by scholars. Soon afterwards Harris reported his acquisition of a papyrus of Homer.[17] But these, and less fascinating fragments, proved insufficient in themselves to kindle the romantic interest for a leap in imagination. Even the announcement, in 1879, that "The Library at Berlin has lately acquired some manuscripts on parchment, portions of the Iliad, Euripides, and Sappho, and some Greek papyri of Aratus obtained in Egypt", apparently suggested little or nothing to most readers.[18]

In 1886 however W. M. Lindsay, who had worked on transcripts of the Herculaneum papyri at Oxford, suggested that scholars should expect major discoveries of classical texts to come from papyri not monasteries:

[T]hose who hoped to hear of great discoveries in the Sinai libraries will be disappointed by the result of Dr. Gardtheusen's exploration, and will be inclined, in view of the wonderful stories about the Fayûm papyri, to look rather to Egypt than to the eastern monasteries for the unearthing of the literary treasures of old.[19]

Only a few years were needed to fulfill his prophecy; and the year 1891 proved to be an *annus mirabilis*. Fragments of the *Antiope* of Euripides were soon succeeded by Aristotle's *Constitution of Athens* and the mimes of Herodas. Other fragments, too, came at last to hand. One writer after the next began to call to mind the era of Petrarch and editiones principes, and to parallel it with his own.[20]

What Lindsay had remarked in a review, what had been hoped in the eighteenth century with the discovery of Herculaneum, now was given sanction by the London *Times* itself:

The hope, which scholars long entertained, that the monasteries of the East might yet give us back the lost decades of Livy, or some of the missing plays of Aeschylus, has gradually faded away as these libraries, one after another, have been examined by European travellers; but as this hope fades another has arisen, and the lovers of classical literature now look, not to Mount Athos or to Constantinople, but to the buried cities and tombs of Egypt. The discovery of manuscripts of classical Greek authors written upon papyrus began less than fifty years ago, and the results obtained since that time have been satisfactory in themselves and still more in the promise which they gave for the future. It is earnestly to be wished, in the interests of all lovers of classical literature, that this may only be the forerunner of many other discoveries of the lost works of the great Greek authors, and that we may yet see again some of the dramas of Aeschylus or Sophocles, of Aristophanes or Menander, which have been lost to the world now for over a thousand years.[21]

In the event, whole plays of Menander were discovered. Substantial additions were made to the texts of Aeschylus, Sophocles, and Aristophanes, but not of them alone. Alcman, Sappho, Archilochus, Timotheus and many other writers have profited by the discoveries. And, as significantly, the thousands of documentary papyri, dating from the third century B.C.E. to the sixth and seventh centuries C.E., have opened home and office and military base to study. Tax laws, police reports, wills, manumission papers, horoscopes, prayers, letters, receipts, charms: it is almost impossible to overstate the amount of new light these documents have shed on our knowledge of antiquity.

In all of this excitement Philodemus and the Fragmenta Herculanensia were not so much forgotten as eclipsed. Naturally, such things had happened before. Sometimes, authors fell out of fashion. For example, the elder Pliny's massive encyclopedia was published fifteen times between 1469 and 1500: the twentieth century has seen not half that number.[22] Now, for over a century, interest in Philodemus was perfunctory. The great Italian edition of the *Herculanensia Volumina quae supersunt* was published only slowly, its first volume appearing at length in 1793, some four decades after the discovery of the papyri themselves.

The second volume was published in 1809; the third volume, eighteen years later.[23] The slowness of publication; the cost of the lavishly produced individual volumes;[24] restrictions on access to the papyri themselves, all of these were not designed to counter the indifferent nature and unpopular sentiments, as it was felt, of the texts. But in the 1860s and 1870s notable scholars, such as Bücheler and Ritschl and Nauck and Gomperz and Cobet, began to write on Philodemus. To be sure, their publications were, in the main, neither numerous nor lengthy: their notes, articles and pamphlets were only *parerga* to these scholars's main interests. Thus, even Theodor Gomperz, whose papers on the Herculanean papyri have lately been re-issued in book-form, cannot be said actually to have centered his interests on Philodemus: to most students, he remains best known for his *Griechische Denker* or *Greek Thinkers*.[25] Later in the nineteenth century, scholars such as Siegfried Sudhaus and Christian Jensen re-edited Philodemean works; students, such as Johannes von Arnim and Hermann Diels and Ulrich von Wilamowitz-Moellendorff, contributed notes or papers to the improvement or elucidation of Philodemean texts; but, here also, the publications were not central to these scholars' labors.

In recent years, however, there has been a considerable increase in interest in Philodemus, and the Herculanean papyri have themselves come to be regarded as worthy of interest in their own right.[26] Nearly a quarter of a century ago, the periodical *Cronache Ercolanesi* was established particularly to treat problems associated with the subject. Introduced by an article by E. G. (later Sir Eric) Turner, its volumes now number well over a score. Numerous books and papers have appeared on the Herculanean papyri and indeed on the history of the excavations, and editions of Philodemus have lately been completed or undertaken.

But, even now, translations of Philodemus are few. Where scores of versions of other classical authors exist, there has been only a handful of attempts to translate works by Philodemus into modern languages. In a sense, this was fortunate. It was as recently as the 1980s that scholars determined that the philosopher's treatises had been originally misreconstructed. Accordingly, both earlier editions and translations were based on a flawed text. New efforts, both to reconstitute Philodemus's text and, through The Philodemus Translation Project, to render his aesthetic works into English, are designed to allow this Epicurean philosopher's language to regain its elegance and his thought its coherence.

THE RECONSTRUCTION OF PHILODEMUS

by

Rebecca Resinski

Upon discovery, the charred and barely recognizable Herculanean papyri could not be unrolled for reading as they would have been in their day. While scholars tried various methods of rendering the scrolls readable, Camillo Paderni and Antonio Piaggio, both beginning work on the papyri in 1753, were responsible for the partial cutting and partial unrolling of Philodemus's texts.[27]

Paderni's cutting of the rolls yielded, ideally, three parts. Two cuts along the length of each roll produced two half-cylinders of papyrus layers with text on the concave side; these layers are known as *scorze*, that is "bark". The central part of the roll, called the *midollo* "marrow", was unsplit by the incisions, lifted out of the cut bark, and unrolled on a special machine engineered by Piaggio.

While the inner *midollo* of a papyrus roll presented continuous columns of writing, the columns on the outer *scorze* were only visible one layer at a time. A layer had to be drawn and then destroyed in order to reach and transcribe the next layer. Draftsmen, chosen for their accuracy as well as their ignorance of Greek,[28] drew the sets of nesting *scorze*. Their drawings are known as *disegni*. Each series of *disegni* for a *scorze* set was numbered; for example, one series belonging to Philodemus's *On Poems* was numbered 460, another 1073. The individual drawings within each series were also numbered as they were drawn (e.g., 460 fragment 1, 460 fr. 2, 460 fr. 3, etc.). The first visible layer—the first one drawn and numbered—was the one closest to the center of the papyrus roll. The last one drawn was the closest to the outside and given the highest number.

Each numbered set of *disegni* represents only one half of the *scorze* layers belonging to a papyrus roll. Unfortunately, the numbers for the sets belonging to the same roll were not necessarily given similar numbers. For example, the 460 and 1073 series belong to the same roll of Philodemus's *On Poems*. Nor were the two *scorze* sets and *midollo* belonging to the same roll catalogued as such.

In the 1980s, Daniel Delattre and Dirk Obbink, independently of each other, reconsidered the process of drafting and destroying subsequent *scorze* layers and so pioneered the method now used for reconstructing the proper order of the Philodemus papyrus rolls.[29]

The drawing, numbering, and destruction of successive *scorze* layers proceeded in opposition to the reading order of a papyrus roll. Usually a reader would begin from the outermost part of the roll and read towards the middle (or interior) of the roll. Draftsmen, on the other hand, worked from the innermost *scorze* to the outermost. In order to make the *disegni* reflect the order of the text, the individually numbered drawings within a set must be rearranged in reverse, numerically descending, order.

Reconstruction is complicated by the fact that each *disegni* series represents, at most, only half of the *scorze* belonging to a roll.[30] Further, the splitting of a roll into only two *scorze* sets is ideal: sometimes lateral fracturing broke the half-cylinders into three or four *scorze* sets. To recreate the outer layers of a Herculanean papyrus roll, a scholar must identify which *disegni* series belong together, reverse the numerical ordering of the drawings within each series, and then interleave the series in descending numerical order. The rearranged drawings of a roll's outer layers must then be matched with the *midollo* belonging to the same roll.

After an order has been established for related *disegni*, the Philodemus texts present other difficulties. Because incisions along a papyrus roll's length could not always correspond to the spaces between columns, some *disegni* depict one or more partial columns of writing which need to be matched with other partial columns. *Disegni* do not always record every successive layer of a roll: some layers stuck to others and could not be separated for transcription. In such cases, a layer may be unrepresented by the *disegni* or a single *disegno* drawing may contain the confused amalgamation of two or more layers. The Philodemus texts were also written without distinctions between upper and lower cases of letters, without breaks between words, and without punctuation—all of which scholars need to add in their modern editions of the texts

The Biblioteca Nazaionale in Naples houses scores of unrolled papyri from Herculaneum. New techniques to treat the rolls are being developed, particularly by a team of Norwegian scholars led by Knut Kleve of the University of Oslo.

NOTES

Mr Naiditch is Publications Editor, Department of Special Collections, and Classics Bibliographer, University Research Library, UCLA; Ms Resinski is a member of the Philodemus Project and the Department of Classics, UCLA.

The authors are most grateful to the Getty Center for the History of Art and the Humanities, Santa Monica (Irene Lotspeich-Phillips, Department of Special Collections), and the Department of Special Collections, Doheny Memorial Library, University of Southern California (Victoria Steele and John Ahouse), for their kindness in making available and in lending materials for this exhibition. Additionally, we desire to thank for their courtesies and aid Gia Aivazian, Librarian for Armenian & Greek, University Research Library, UCLA; John Bidwell, William Andrews Clark Library, UCLA; David Blank, Department of Classics, UCLA; Mark Brown, John Hay Library, Brown University, Providence, Rhode Island; Anne Caiger, Department of Special Collections, UCLA; Jonnie A. Hargis, Reference/Acquisitions, UCLA Map Library; Michael W. Haslam and Richard Janko, Department of Classics, UCLA; Sue A. Kaplan, Department of Special Collections, URL, UCLA; and Michael M. Noga, Head, Geology-Geophysics Library, UCLA; the UCLA Arts Library and the UCLA Music Library.

Finally, we desire to give thanks to the Bernadine J. L. M. Zelenka Endowment for aid in producing this catalogue.

[1] *The Travels of Lord Charlemont in Greece & Turkey 1749* edited by W. B. Stanford and E. J. Finopoulos, London: Trigraph-London for the A. G. Leventis Foundation, 1984, p. 42.

[2] A. C. de la Mare, *The Handwriting of the Italian Humanists* 1.1, Oxford: for the Association internationale de bibliophilie, 1973, p. 5.

[3] Texts established in the fifteenth century were, unfortunately, often too firmly based on mediocre manuscripts: see E. J. Kenney, *The Classical Text: Aspects of Editing in the Age of the Printed Book*, Berkeley/Los Angeles 1974, pp. 1 sqq.

[4] Cf. "Augustan Manetho" *Liverpool Classical Monthly* 14, 1989, pp. 105 sq.

[5] Anon., *Some Account of the Roman History by Fabius Pictor; From a Manuscript lately discover'd in Herculaneum; the Underground City near Naples*, London: Printed for M. Cooper, 1749 (William Andrews Clark Library, UCLA, Coll. Pam.).

[6] For a detailed account of the discovery of papyri at Herculaneum, see Michele Ruggiero, *Storia degli scavi di Ercolano*, Naples 1885, pp. xliii-xlv, 124 sq., 132-134, 149, 154, 156 sq., 159 sq. For a general account, identifying the role of Maria Amalia, see G. W. Bowersock, "The Rediscovery of Herculaneum and Pompeii" *The American Scholar* 47.4, Autumn 1978, pp. 461-70.

[7] Cf. *The Travels of the Learned Father Montfaucon from Paris thro' Italy . . . made English from the Paris Edition*, London: Printed by D. L. for E. Curll [etc.], 1712, p. 73: "Hence we proceeded to see the Manuscript of the Gospel of St. *Mark*, which is kept in a Cupboard hard by, and we view'd it to Content with D. *Leith*, or *Galterius* the Library-Keeper: It is a square Book, with a gilt Silver Cover, made of the *Egyptian Papyrus*". It is

held by some however that papyri circulated widely after 1500 (A. Grafton, *Journal of the Warburg and Courtauld Institutes* 42, 1979, p. 168). For early discussions of papyri, see J. A. Fabricius/P. Schaffshausen, *Bibliotheca Antiquaria*, Hamburg 1760 ed. 3, p. 957.

[8] Anon., *Some Account of the Roman History by Fabius Pictor* p. 6.

[9] Anon., *The Scots Magazine* 16, May 1754, pp. 243 sq.

[10] See below nos. 22-24. See also "Notes on the History of British Papyrology II: the Development of Papyrology in Great Britain to 1896" *LCM* 17, 1992, p. 71 n. 4.

[11] *Journal of a Tour to Italy*, Dublin 1763, pp. 68 sq.

[12] Le Chevalier de Jaucourt, "Herculaneum" *Encyclopédie ou dictionnaire raisonné des sciences, des arts études métiers* 8, Neufchastel 1765, p. 153. See also *LCM* 17, 1992, p. 71 n. 5.

[13] Anon., *The Scots Magazine* 17, Aug. 1755, p. 397; W. Gell/John P. Gandy, *Pompeiana: the Topography, Edifices, and Ornaments of Pompeii*, London 1817/1819, p. xv; Anon., *Athenaeum* no. 1014, April 3, 1847, p. 361. The papyri were preserved at Portici (see A. Allroggen-Bedel/H. Kammerer-Grothaus, "Das Museo Ercolanese in Portici" *Cronache Ercolanese* 10, 1980, pp. 175-217). There, they became a tourist attraction. Even so, some visitors did not trouble even to record their viewing of the papyri ("A Journal kept by Mr Tracy and Mr Dentand, during their Travels through France and Italy", 1766, p. 67 [Bodleian Library, Ms. Add. a 366]; "The Journal of the Right Hon[ble] Sir William Drummond", Sept. 29, 1787 [Yale University, Beinecke Library, Osborn Shelves c 331]; Mariana Starke, *Travels in Italy between the Years 1792 and 1798*, 2, London 1802, pp. 117-129). Of those who refer to the Herculanean papyri, some show themselves as interested, if indeed not more interested, in the mechanisms developed for unrolling the papyri than in the papyri themselves: see John Waldie, "A Journal of Travels 37, Feb. 14, 1817, p. 374 (below no. 26); Miss Tempest, "Visit to Italy 1816-1818" (Nov. 29, 1817: Yale, Beinecke, Osborn Shelves d 166); John Grant, "Journal of Travel in Italy", Dec. 16, 1817-April 30, 1818, 4 p. 46 (Boston Public Library Ms f Am 1227). An anonymous diarist, having recorded his hope that Tacitus, Livy and Cicero might still be found in Herculaneum were proper excavations undertaken, turns to describing the techniques for unrolling the papyri (Yale, Beinecke, Osborn d 288 v. 2 f. 25 [1821]).

[14] N. Horsfall, *Greek, Roman, and Byzantine Studies* 15, 1974, p. 475.

[15] Davy had reported that of 1696 manuscripts he judged only 80-120 were both unrollable and legible (*Philosophical Transactions of the Royal Society 1821* v. I pp. 191-207; cf. *Gentleman's Magazine* 89.1, May 1819, pp. 446 sq.). For Davy, see below no. 37. B. Fosse, K. Kleeve and F. C. Störmer note that there are 2007 items; that 1320 remain to be opened; and that a new method of unrolling the papyri may make half of them accessible (*Cronache Ercolanese* 14, 1984, pp. 9-15). See also K. Kleve et al., "Three Technical Guides to the Papyri of Herculaneum" *CE* 21, 1991, pp. 111-24. For a census of the papyri, see M. Gigante, *Catalogo dei papiri ercolanensi*, Naples 1979. On additional problems in reconstruction, see E. G. Turner, "Sniffing Glue" *CE* 13, 1983, pp. 7-14.

[16] *Charta Papyracea Graece scripta Musei Borgiani Velitris qua series incolarum Ptolemaidis Arsinoiticae in aggeribus et fossis operantium exhibetur,* Romae: apud Antonium Fulgonium, 1788, pp. III-IV (Harvard University, Widener Library, Arc. Gp 11 45):

> Reperta fuit charta papyracea Musei Borgiani una cum quadraginta aut quinquaginta aliis anno MDCCLXXVIII. in loco quodam subterraneo urbis Gizae, in cuius regione, ut notum est, antiqua Memphis vulgo sita esse creditur. Omnes hae chartae papyraceae [quonam modo volutae fuerint nescio] in capsula quadam ex ligno sycomori reconditae, negotiatori cuidam exiguo pretio offerebantur: hic autem summi harum rerum valoris ac pretii nescius, unam tantum, quae nostra est, novitatis causa emptam ad amplissimum Praesulem Stephanum Borgiam mittendam curabat: reliquias diripiebant Turcae, earumque fumo [nam odorem fumi aromaticum esse dicunt] sese oblectabant.

The work itself is scarce and, even in its own time, does not appear to have circulated widely (cf. *LCM* 17, 1992, p. 73 n. 17). Even Richard Porson himself probably did not own Schow's *Charta Papyracea Graece*: the work has no place in the auction, nor in the group sold to Trinity, nor among such few volumes as Porson is known to have otherwise acquired but seemingly did not retain. The earliest reference to Schow in scholarly literature that chances to have come my way appears in W. Adolph Schimdt, *Die Griechischen Papyruskunden der königlichen Bibliothek zu Berlin*, Berlin 1842, p. [vii], though it would not surprise me were there earlier references. For the controversy about the odor of papyri, see E. G. Turner, *Greek Papyri*, Oxford 1968, p. 19.

[17] See *Athen.* 1053, Jan. 1, 1848, p. 15; *ibid.* 1206, Dec. 7, 1850, p. 1281 (cf. *LCM* 16, 1991, pp. 72 sq.). It is to be noted that, even in England, there were then classical periodicals (see *The Cambridge Ritualists Reconsidered* ed. W. M. Calder III, Atlanta 1991, pp. 130-134. Curiously, W. H. de Vriese's "Essay on the Papyrus of the Ancients", translated by W. B. Macdonald, included no references to the Herculanean papyri (*Classical Museum* 5.2, 1847, pp. 202-215).

[18] *Athen.* 2716, Nov. 15, 1879, p. 633.

[19] *Academy* 30, Dec. 4, 1886, p. 382. For Lindsay's work on the papyri, see W. Scott, *Fragmenta Herculanensia*, Oxford 1885; *Thirty-Six Engravings of Texts and Alphabets from the Herculanean Fragments taken from the Original Copperplates executed under the Direction of the Rev. John Hayter*, Oxford 1891 (Indiana University, Bloomington, University Library PA 3317 A1 1891 oversize).

[20] R. C. Jebb, *Journal of Hellenic Studies* 12, 1891, pp. xliv sq.; W. L. Newman, *Classical Review* 5, April 1891, p. 155; F. G. Kenyon, *CR* 6, July 1892, p. 285; Anon., *Athen.* 3925, Jan. 17, 1903, p. 75a.

[21] *Times* Jan. 19, 1891, p. 9.

[22] At present, when at any one time dozens of students might have in hand theses or dissertations on Ovid, it is rare for more than a few to be working on Pliny: see Anon., *A Draft Index of Dissertations and Theses in the Classics and Related Subjects in Progress or Recently Completed in North America and Great Britain*, Los Angeles: UCLA Special

Collections, 1992, pp. 48-50 (33 theses and dissertations in progress or completed on Ovid; one dissertation in progress on Pliny).

[23] The remaining volumes (IV-VI, VIII-XI) appeared respectively in 1832, 1843, 1839, 1844, 1848, 1850, 1855; volume VII was never issued. See *Classical Journal* 66, June 1826, p 358; cf. W. Engelmann/E. Preuss, *Bibliotheca scriptorum classicorum* 1, Leipzig 1880, pp. 45 sq.

[24] Porson owned a copy of volume I (*A Catalogue of Part of the Library of the late Richard Porson*, London: Leigh & Sotheby, June 16, 1809, no. 593). At the auction, it brought £5/15/6, and thus as much or more than some 97% of the other lots. Its price, to give it context, is similar to that given for the editio princeps of Aristophanes (Venice: Aldus, 1498: £5/5 no. 176); for Herodotus (Rome 1474: £5 no. 594; now Trinity College, Cambridge, Grylls 2:128); and for Hemsterhuys's Lucian of 1743 (£5/12/6 no. 741). The first two volumes of the *Volumina* were said in 1819 to be available in Naples for five dollars each (Usher Parsons, letter, June 10, 1819: Brown University, John Hay Library, Ms. 77.10 box 8 folder 29, kindly brought to my attention by Mark Brown).

[25] Theodor Gomperz, *Eine Auswahl herkulanischer kleiner Schriften (1864-1909)* herausg. T. Dorandi, Leiden: E. J. Brill, 1993.

[26] Such shifts in interest are of course not unknown in the history of scholarship or *Rezeptionsgeschichte*. Greek tragedy for example excited at first relatively little interest: Aeschylus, though first published in 1518, was not translated into vernacular languages until over 250 years had passed. Sophocles, edited in 1502, was not rendered into English until 1729 and French until 1785. Euripides, whose complete works were first published in 1503, was not translated into English or French until the early 1780s. True, there were Latin translations, dating respectively to 1555, 1543 and 1541. But their relevance to the argument is minimal because Seneca, who wrote his tragedies in Latin, was rendered into Italian in 1560; into English in 1581; into French in 1664; and indeed into Polish in 1696 (*The British Library General Catalogue of Printed Books to 1975* vol. 298, London 1985, pp. 115-118).

[27] Mario Capasso, *Manuale di papirologia ercolanese*, Lecce: Congedo 1992. Capasso details the attempts to read the papyrus rolls.

[28] Chief among these draftsmen were G. B. Casanova, F. Cenlantano, and G. Malesci. Their ignorance of Greek was presumed to guarantee their pure perception and recording of the literal remains.

[29] Daniel Delattre, "Philodème, *De la musique*: livre IV, colonnes 40* à 109*" *Cronache Ercolanesi* 19, 1989, pp. 49-143; Dirk Obbink, *Philodemus: De Pietate I*, Dissertation: Stanford University 1986

[30] This paragraph and the next, which both list complications encountered in reconstruction using the Delattre/Obbink method, follow Richard Janko, "Philodemus Resartus: Progress in Reconstructing the Philosophical Papyri from Herculaneum" *Proceedings of the Boston Area Colloquium in Ancient Philosophy* 7, 1991, pp. 271-308.

ITALY AND THE BAY OF NAPLES

Case I

1. [Italy] *L'Italie. Dressée sur les observations de l'académie des sciences par Guil. Delisle. Nouvellement revue et augmentee* [sic] *par Dezauche*, Paris 1817. **An overview of Italy as a whole.

   UCLA Special Collections coll. 931 box 49 (Stuart de Rothesay Maps).

2. [The Bay of Naples.] Sir William Hamilton, *Observations on Mount Vesuvius, Mount Etnœ, and other Volcanoes: in a Series of Letters*, London: Printed for T. Cadell, 1774 **Map of the region around the Gulf of Naples. Vesuvius, Naples, and Portici are marked.

   UCLA Geology Library QE 527.H18o (Locked Case).

3. [Vesuvius.] Anon., *The Natural History of Mount Vesuvius . . . translated from the Original Italian*, London: Printed for E. Cave, 1743. **Plate showing the *"Prospect of* Vesuvius *from the King's Palace at* Portici" nine years before the discovery of the Villa dei Papiri.

   UCLA Geology Library QE 523.V65 4liE (Locked Case)

4. [Vesuvius.] John Phillips, *Vesuvius*, Oxford: Clarendon Press, 1869. **Map of lava flows and ash falls from the volcano, with Portici, Pompeii etc. marked.

   UCLA Geology Library QE 523 V6 P5 (Locked Case).

5. [Vesuvius.] L. Housman, *A. E. H.: Some Poems, Some Letters and a Personal Memoir*, London 1937, p. 134. **The poet and classical scholar A. E. Housman, who contributed corrections to papyri of Euripides, Bacchylides, Callimachus and others, made an excursion to Naples in 1897. In the present letter he describes his visit to Vesuvius.

   > When you get to the cone you begin to hear an angry sound such as water will sometimes make in pipes, as if the mountain were gargling, or were trying to talk but had stones in its mouth; which indeed it has . . . There had been an overflow about a month before I was there . . . I went to the place: the surface had mostly turned grey, but the red-hot part could be seen through cracks, and the heat in some places was like a furnace. The guides fasten coins to the end of long sticks, plunge them into these cracks, and withdraw them with the hot lava adhering to them. .

   UCLA URL PR 4809.H15 H8.

13

HERCULANEUM

Case II

6. [Destruction of Herculaneum and Pompeii.] C. *Plini Secundi Nouocomensis, Epistolarum libri X* [etc], Parisiis: ex officina Rob. Stephani, 152[8]. **The younger Pliny provides the only eye-witness account of the eruption of Vesuvius in 79 C.E. In the present letter, written at the behest of his friend the historian Tacitus, he explains how his uncle the elder Pliny set out first to investigate the eruption and then to render assistance to victims, and was himself overcome by fumes at Stabiae.

> UCLA Special Collections PA 6638 A2 1529. From the library of Jean Bouhier (1655-1735), Seigneur de Versalieu.

7. *Pliny's Epistles and Panegyrick translated by Several Hands, with the Life of Pliny by Mr Henley,* London: Printed for W. Mears, 1724.

> A Cloud arose (it was uncertain, at a Distance, from what Mountain, tho' it appear'd after to be Vesuvius) in Likeness and Form resembling a Pine-Tree; for it was elevated to a good Height, with a long Trunk, and distributed in several Branches. The Reason, I suppose, was, that it was rais'd aloft by a sudden Wind, and then relinquish'd by it, as it decay'd, or else overpower'd by its own Weight, it spread it self into a large Breadth; appearing sometimes white, sometimes Shadowy, and variously colour'd, as it was loaded with Ashes or with Earth. It struck him [*viz.* the elder Pliny] with Surprize, and seem'd to merit a nearer Examination. He orders a light frigate to be fitted out, and gives me leave, if I thought proper, to go along with him. I answer'd him, that I was rather inclin'd to Study, and by a great Hazard, he had deliver'd something to me, in order to be transcrib'd. He parted from his House, and Table-Book with him. The Sea-Officers at *Retina,* alarm'd at the impending Danger (for that Village was exactly below *Misenum,* nor was there any way to escape but by Sea,) importun'd him to prevent so terrible a Disaster. He would not alter his Resolution, but pursu'd with the utmost Courage, what he had enter'd upon with an eager Curiosity. He draws out the Gallies, and goes on Board himself, with a Design to give Succour not only to Retina, but to many other Places. . . . [At Stabiae,] he gives Orders to be convey'd to the Bath; after Bathing, he sits down to Supper chearfully, or, what is equal, with all the Appearance of the ordinary Gaiety. In the mean time, large and high Eruptions of Fire glar'd from Mount Vesuvius in several Places, the Brightness of which was heightened by the Gloom of the Night. . . . . [T]he Buildings were shock'd by violent and repeated Earthquakes, and seem'd to rock on one Side and the other, as if they had been mov'd from their Foundations. Abroad, the Fall of the Pumice-Stones, tho' light and eaten thro', alarm'd them. . . . [To] guard against the fall of the Stones, they ty'd each of them a Pillow about their Heads with handkerchiefs or Napkins. It was now Day in other Places, but there it was still Night, more black and dismal than ever was known, but it was something dissipated by a multitude of Lights and Flambeaux. They thought it proper to advance to the Shore, and examine more nearly, as far as the Sea allow'd them, which still ran high, and was ruffled with a contrary Wind. There my Uncle lying down upon a Sheet that was spread under him, ask'd once or twice for Water, and took a Draught of it; soon after, the Flames, and a stench of Sulphur, a

fore-runner of the Flames, dispersed all the Company; and rous'd him. He got up supported by two Servants, and at that Moment, fell and expir'd.

Private Collection.

8. [Excavations at Herculaneum.] Joseph Jay Deiss, *Herculaneum: Italy's Buried Treasure*, revised and updated edition, New York: Harper & Row, 1985, p. 34. **Aerial photograph of the excavated portions of Herculaneum, with archaeological map below.

UCLA URL X2 538 426.

9. Amedeo Maiuri, *Pompei, Ercolano e Stabia: Le città sepolte dal Vesuvio*, Novara: Istituto geografico de Agostino, 1961. **The entrance to the Theatre of Herculaneum.

UCLA URL *DG 70P7 M28.

10. [Herculaneum: Villa dei Papiri.] Domenico Mustilli et al., *Villa dei papiri*, Naples 1983, pp. 8-9. **The Villa dei Papiri was originally excavated by Karl Weber, whose plan of the villa is shown.

UCLA URL *DG 70 H5V55 1983.

11. [Herculaneum: Villa of the Papyri at Malibu.] Norman Neuerburg, *Herculaneum to Malibu: a Companion to the Visit of the J. Paul Getty Museum*, Malibu: Museum 1975. **Neuerburg's reconstruction of the Villa dei Papiri.

UCLA Arts Library *N582 N394h.

12. [Herculaneum: art work] [Howard Loxton], *Pompeii and Herculaneum*, London: Spring Books, 1966, pp. 152-153. **Bronze sculpture from the Villa of the Papyri.

Private Collection.

13. Theodor Kraus / Leonard von Matt (photographer), *Pompeii and Herculaneum: the Living Cities of the Dead*, translated by Robert Erich Wolf, New York: Harry N. Abrams Inc., 1973, plates 213-214. **Representations of Pompeiians with writing materials. On the left (plate 213), an unknown woman from the time of Claudius (41-54); on the right (plate 214), Terentius Neo and his wife (time of Vespasian, 69-79). The women hold wax tablets and styli; Neo, a roll.

UCLA URL *N 5769 K868pE.

PAPYRI

Case III

14. *Caii Plynii Secundi naturalis historiae libri tricesimiseptimi,* Venice: Nicolaus Jenson, 1472. **The elder Pliny (ca 23-79), who was killed whilst bringing aid to the victims of Vesuvius, was the author of an encyclopedia. The present edition, the third to appear, is opened to the beginning of book XIII. Later in this book appears an account of the manufacture of papyri.

UCLA Special Collections **A 1 P71h 1472.

15. *The Historie of the World commonly called, the Naturall Historie of C. Plinius Secundus.* Translated into English by Philemon Holland, London: Printed by Adam Islip, 1601, pp. 392 sq. ** The first complete translation of Pliny's *Naturalis Historia* into English, turned to Book XIII Chap. XII: "Of divers kinds of Paper: and how writing Paper is made: also the triall of good or bad Paper: and the glue or past belonging thereto".

UCLA Special Collections *PA 6612 P71h v. 1.

16. T. S. Pattie / E. G. Turner, *The Written Word on Papyrus: an Exhibition held in The British Museum 30 July - 27 October 1974,* [London:] Published for The British Library Board by British Museum Publications Limited, 1974, p. 23. **The ninth plate displays an unopened papyrus roll.

Private Collection.

17. E. G. Turner, *Greek Manuscripts of the Ancient World,* Oxford: Clarendon Press, 1971, pp. 30-31: "Construction of a Sheet of Papyrus"; "Cell Structure of Stem of Papyrus Plant"; "Fibre Structure of a Sheet of Papyrus".

Private Collection.

18. Specimen Greek papyrus. Unidentified documentary text tentatively assigned to s. VI.

UCLA Special Collections Ms. 170/646.

19. Roger A. Pack, *The Greek and Latin Literary Texts from Greco-Roman Egypt,* Ann Arbor: The University of Michigan Press, 1967. **The second and last edition of a work, first published in 1952, that presents in convenient form a bibliographical listing of discoveries from the nineteenth and twentieth centuries. A third edition, bringing the material up to date, is a great desideratum, and Paul Mertens, Seminaire de papyrologie, Université de Liège, has a third edition in hand.

Private Collection. Annotations in this copy signal papyri near in date to the time of their authors, and to the replacement of the papyrus roll by the papyrus or parchment codex.

20. Jean Lenaerts / Paul Mertens, "Les papyrus d'Isocrate" *Chronique d'Égypte* 64, 1989, pp. 216-230. **Offprint illustrating the manner of presentation adopted for *Catalogue des papyrus littéraires grecs et latins*, the third edition of Pack (in preparation).

21. [Forgery.] *Bibliotheca Philippica: Catalogue of Greek and Italian Manuscripts and English Charters from the Celebrated Collection) formed by Sir Thomas Phillipps, Bt. (1792-1872)*, New Series: Eighth Part, London: Sotheby & Co., July 4, 1972, no. 1724. **Reproduction of roll of Homer, allegedly dating to 83 B.C.E., written on parchment in square capitals (by the forger Constantine Simonides)

THE DISCOVERY OF PAPYRI AT HERCULANEUM

Case IV

22. Camillo Paderni, letter to Dr Mead, Nov. 18, 1752 (*The Monthly Review, or, Literary Journal* 11, 1754, p. 214, reprinting the text from the *Philosophical Transactions*):

> It is not a month ago, that there have been found many volumes of papirus, but turned to a sort of charcoal, so brittle, that, being touched, it falls readily into ashes. Nevertheless, by his majesty's orders, I have made some trials to open them, but all to no purpose; excepting some words, which I have picked out entire, where there are divers *bits*, by which it appears in what manner the whole was written. The form of the characters, made with a very black tincture, that overcomes the darkness of the charcoal, I shall here, to oblige you, in two short lines; my fidelity to the king not permitting me to send you any more.

23. Camillo Paderni, to T(homa)s H(olli)s, Oct. 18, 1754 (*The Gentleman's Magazine* 25, 1755, p. 21):

> As yet we have only entered into one room [under the wood belonging to the church of the Augustinians], the floor of which is formed of Mosaic work, not unelegant. It appears to have been a library adorned with presses, inlaid with different sorts of wood, disposed in rows, at the top of which were cornishes, as in our own times. I was buried in this spot more than 12 days, to carry off the volumes found there, many of which were so perished, that it was impossible to remove them. Those which I took away amounted to the number of 337, all of them at present incapable of being opened: These are all written in *Greek* characters. While I was busy in this work, I observed a large bundle, which, from the size, I imagined must contain more than a single volume: I tried with the utmost care to get it out, but could not, from the damp and weight of it. However, I perceived that it consisted of about 18 volumes. . . . All these were written in Latin, as appears by a

few words which broke off from them. I was in hopes to have got something out of them, but they are in a worse condition than the Greek. From the latter the public will see some entire columns, having myself had the good fortune to extract two, and many other fine fragments. Of all these an account is drawing up, which will be published together with the other Greek characters, now engraving on copper plates, and afterwards make a separate work by themselves. . . . Those which I have opened are philosophical tracts, the subjects of which are known to me, but I am not at liberty to be more explicit: When they are published, they shall be immediately conveyed to you.

UCLA URL AP 4G28 1755.

24. Anon. Neapolitanus, to Monsignor Cerati, Feb. 25, 1755 (*The Critical Review: or, Annals of Literature* 2, London 1756, reprinted from the *Philosophical Transactions for the Year 1755*):

In obedience to your commands, I send you the best account I can of the writings. You must know then, that within two years last past, in a chamber of a house, (or more properly speaking, of an antient villa, . . .) there has been found a great quantity of rolls, about half a palm long, and round; which appeared like roots of wood, all black, and seeming to be only of one piece. One of them falling on the ground, it broke in the middle, and many letters were observed, by which it was first known, that the rolls were of papyrus. The number of these rolls, as I am told, were about 150, of different sizes.

UCLA URL AP 4 C87 v. 2.

25. Henry Penruddock Wyndham, "Notes of a Tour" (manuscript diary: April 1766). **Account of a visit to Herculaneum by the travel-writer Wyndham (1736-1819):

There is a method found out of unrolling these manuscripts, & as they are written only on one side they tho' with difficulty are able to transcribe them; there is a machine on purpose. I was told, the Manuscripts are all Greek: but those few which already have been interpreted, have been found of very little consequence.

UCLA Special Collections coll. 170/16 v. 6.

26. John Waldie, *A Journal of Travels* vol. 37 p. 374 (manuscript diary: Feb. 14, 1817):

We then went to the Studio where was formerly the university of Naples, now it is the Museum for the reception of the Pictures & Statues &c. of the King. – We went to see the Papiri or Manuscripts from Herculaneum. They are most curious – and quite a soft black tinder – yet held to the light are legible, tho' much broken & injured. Some are Greek & some Latin – There are nearly 320 already unfolded, & besides these are a great many more near 1400. The unrolling is the work of much time & labor – & done by a small sort of frame & ribbons & gradually as they are unfolded bits of gold-beater's skin are pasted on the back of them. By this means several have been got quite perfect – a treatise on Music by Philodemus is the best thing there has been found.

UCLA Special Collections Ms. 169/26.

18

27. Charles Waldstein / Leonard Shoobridge, *Herculaneum: Past, Present, & Future*, London 1908, pp. 8-9.

No doubt we have all been rejoiced by the rich harvest of important manuscripts which have of late years been discovered in Egypt, where the nature of the soil favours the best preservation of these delicate objects. Our hopes have been justly raised that the future may have further important additions to ancient literature in store for us from this quarter. ... Here [however] in one villa about 800 manuscripts were found together forming the library of one man. Unfortunately, the possessor of this villa was a specialist and not a man of all-round culture; ... But all the rich dwellers in the villas of Herculaneum were not such specialists; and should we come upon the library of an ordinary lady or gentleman of the age, we may certainly expect to find the classical representatives of ancient thought and literary art. All the great tragedians or writers of comedy (including Menander) may be there waiting for us in their completeness. The works of the early Greek philosophers, Heracleitus, Parmenides, Empedocles, Democritus, Anaxagoras, and all the treasure of thought only known to us from fragmentary lines in later writers; the missing works of Plato and Aristotle (what would one not give to see a complete *Poetics*?); the whole of Roman literature, the lost books of Livy,—one hardly dares to allow one's imagination to roam in these dazzling fields of classical light.

UCLA URL N 5775 W16h.

28. *Dr. Burney's Musical Tours in Europe. Volume I: An Eighteenth-Century Musical Tour in France and Italy* ed. Percy A. Scholes, London: Oxford University Press, 1959.

Mr Hamilton ... says nothing is allowed to be copied at Portici, & not a pencil suffered to appear there, and of him the Neapolitans are more suspicious and jealous than of any one else. I wished very much to have a bit of the Greek MS. recovered on Music, though a Satire against it, but till the court publishes it, nothing can be obtained, no more than of the entire ancient instruments found in Herculaneum, and Pompeij.

UCLA Music Library ML 195 B93p 1959.

29. *Herculanensium voluminum quæ supersunt tomus I-II*, Neapoli: ex regia typographia, 1793, 1809. **Both the editio princeps of Philodemus and the first publication of the Herculaneum papyri.

Lent by the Getty Center for the Study of the Arts and the Humanities, Santa Monica, Department of Special Collections 84-B30790 (oversize).

30. Rev. John Hayter, *A Report upon the Herculaneum Manuscripts, in a Second Letter, addressed, by Permission, to His Royal Highness the Prince Regent*, London: Printed for Richard Phillips, 1811. **Includes "A New Editio of the First Letter" (p. [113]).

Lent by the Getty Center for the Study of the Arts and the Humanities, Santa Monica, Department of Special Collections 84-B30619 (oversize).

THE RECONSTRUCTION OF PHILODEMUS

Case V

31. F. C. Störmer, I. Lorentzen, B. Fosse, M. Capasso, K. Kleve, "Ink in Herculaneum" in *Cronache Ercolanesi: bollettino del centro internazionale per lo studio dei papiri ercolanesi* vol. 20, 1990, p. 183.

> Lent by Richard Janko.

32. Philodemi περὶ ποιημάτων libri secundi quae videntur ¹fragmenta conlegit restituit inlustravit Augustus Hausrath, Lipsiae: in aedibus B. G. Teubneri, 1889. **Annotated by Theodor Gomperz (1832-1912) whose classical library, together with that of his son Heinrich, was acquired by the University of Southern California.

> Lent by the University of Southern California, Department of Special Collections, PA 4271 P3P4 1889.

33. Theodor Gomperz, autograph letter, signed, to Sir Richard Claverhouse Jebb, Oct. 4, 1905. **Acknowledging a copy of Jebb's edition of Bacchylides.

> UCLA Special Collections Ms. 100/67 folder III (R. C. Jebb Papers).

34. Siegfried Sudhaus, editor, *Philodemi volumina rhetorica*, Lipsiae: in aedibus B. G. Teubneri, 1892, 1895, 1896. Three volumes. **This set belonged to the German classical scholar Karl Praechter, who published on Philodemus.

> Private Collection.

35. Facsimile of layers of the Herculanean papyri. **Transparencies of *disegni* from the 460 series arranged to illustrate their relative positioning in the *scorze* layers. The draftsman of these *disegni*, G. B. Casanova, worked on this series in 1821 and 1822. Drawing and stripping away fragments 19 and 20 first, he then drew and destroyed the next two layers, containing fragments 21 through 24. Reconstructing the papyrus roll from which these *disegni* come involves reversing the numerical order of the fragment drawings and interleaving this series with the 1073 series (the other half of this roll's *scorze*) also rearranged in decreasing numerical order. Of the fragments exhibited here, fragment 24 is the closest to the beginning (or outside) of the papyrus roll, while fragment 19 is closest to the roll's end (or, when rolled, its middle)

> Lent by Richard Janko.

36. [Piaggio's machine for unrolling the Herculanean papyri.] Mario Capasso, *Storia fotographica dell' officina dei papiri ercolanesi*, [Naples] 1983. **Tav. 50: "Schema della machina del Piaggio da G. Castrucci (1852)".

> UCLA URL PA 3317 C37 1983.

37. [Sir Humphry Davy's efforts to unroll the Herculanean Papyri.] *Italy* by Lady de Morgan vol. 2, London: Henry Colburn and Co., 1821.

> In this room we visited Sir Humphry Davy, who was employed in unrolling the manuscripts which, reduced to a state of charcoal by the eruption, have thus been preserved for modern inspection. There has been already unrolled a Treatise on Music, by Philodemus; two books of Epicurus, and the fragments of an heroic poem attributed to Rabirius. Most of the seventeen hundred manuscripts found in Herculaneum, are, it is said, capable of being unrolled. Those which are daily found in Pompeii are reduced to dust by humidity, and are beyond recal.

UCLA Special Collections DG 426 M823i.

38. Photographs of papyri from Herculaneum.

UCLA Department of Classics / UCLA Special Collections.

GRAECO–ROMAN EGYPT AND EARLY DISCOVERIES

Wall Case I

39. [Map of Egypt] Naphtali Lewis, *Life in Egypt under Roman Rule*, Oxford: Clarendon Press, 1983, pp. 230-231. **Lewis's map includes the locations of many sites at which papyri were discovered: Hermopolis, Antinoopolis, Oxyrhynchus, Tebtunis, Karanis etc.

Private Collection.

40. [Plan of Karanis.] Elinor M. Husselman, *Karanis Excavations of the University of Michigan in Egypt 1928-1935: Topography and Architecture. A Summary of the Reports of the Director, Enoch E. Peterson*, Ann Arbor: The University of Michigan Press, 1979. [Map 11].

UCLA Arts *DT 73 K33 H87.

41. [Plan of Oxyrhynchus.] *The Oxyrhynchus Papyri volume L* edited with Translations by A. K. Bowman et al., London: Published for the British Academy by the Egypt Exploration Society, 1983, pp. vi-vii. **A. S. Hunt's "The Damping out and flattening of Papyri" and a "Plan of Oxyrhynchus". The volume itself includes fragments of Menander, Theocritus, Vergil (s. I), and John's Gospel (s. II).

UCLA URL *PA 3315 09 v. 50.

42. Sir Eric Turner, "The Graeco-Roman Branch", *Excavating in Egypt: the Egypt Exploration Society 1881-1982* edited by T. G. H. James, Chicago: University of Chicago Press, 1982 (1984) p. 160. **Photograph of "Grenfell and Hunt at Oxyrhynchus"

UCLA URL DT 56.9 E96 1982.

43. Joseph Arden / Rev. Churchill Babington, *ΥΠΕΡΙΔΟΥ ΛΟΓΟΙ Β. The Orations of Hyperides for Lycophron and for Euxenippus; now first Printed in Facsimile with a Short Account of the Discovery of the Original Manuscript at Western Thebes in Upper Egypt in 1847*, Cambridge: Printed at the University Press, 1853.

CLASSICAL TEXTS FROM ANTIQUITY

Wall Case II

44. F. G. Kenyon, *Classical Texts from Papyri in the British Museum including the Newly Discovered Poems of Herodas*, London: Printed by Order of the Trustees of the British Museum, 1891. **The editio princeps of Herodas. The volume also includes works by Demosthenes, Isocrates, Homer and perhaps Hyperides and Tryphon.

45. Walter Headlam, *Herodas: the Mimes and Fragments* edited by A. D. Knox, Cambridge: University Press, 1922. **It was one of Headlam's chief ambitions to complete an edition of Herodas but, unfortunately, he died young in 1908, and Knox, perhaps best remembered today for his work in deciphering codes during the two world wars, brought the volume to fruition.

46. Penelope Fitzgerald, *The Knox Brothers*, New York: Coward, McCann & Geoghegan, 1977, facing page 192. **Portrait of A. D. Knox ("Dilly" by Gilbert Spencer; photograph of papyrus of Herodas)

47. F. G. Kenyon, editor, *ΑΘΗΝΑΙΩΝ ΠΟΛΙΤΕΙΑ: Aristotle on the Constitution of Athens*, London: Printed by Order of the Trustees of the British Museum, 1891. **The *editio princeps* of one of the first major discoveries to capture the imagination of scholars. This copy belonged to Albert Charles Clauson (1870-1946), later first Baron Clauson, who has added a note: "Bought Feb 13th 1891: original price 7/6, but 10/- paid for this copy as it was one of the last copies of the edition, one of the few 'editiones principes' of modern times" (p. [i]).

48. *ΑΘΗΝΑΙΩΝ ΠΟΛΙΤΕΙΑ. Aristotle on the Constitution of Athens. Facsimile of Papyrus CXXXI in the British Museum*, London: Printed by Order of the Trustees of the British Museum, 1891. **First edition.

49. *Trinity College Lecture Room*, Nov. 3, 1893. **Texts for translation from Greek and Latin into English or from English into Greek or Latin from Trinity College, Cambridge. The student is advised that "This fragment was recently published from an Egyptian papyrus" and instructed to "Emend the text where corruption is indicated; and discuss the authorship, taking into account metre and style". On the following leaf, to show how the work should be done, J. D. Duff translates the fragments and discusses their authorship.

Private Collection.

50. Bernard P. Grenfell / Arthur S. Hunt, *ΛΟΓΙΑ ΙΗΧΟΥ: Sayings of Our Lord from an Early Greek Papyrus*, Published for the Egypt Exploration Fund by Henry Frowde, 1897. **This papyrus was later re-issued as P. Oxy. vol. 1 no. I. It was translated by M. R. James, best known for his work as a Latin palaeographer and writer of ghost stories, in *The Apocryphal New Testament*, 1924: Oxford 1975, pp. 26-28.

UCLA URL BS 2970 A72 1897.

51. *The Poems of Bacchylides from a Papyrus in the British Museum* edited by Frederic G. Kenyon, London: Printed by Order of the Trustees of the British Museum, 1897. **Annotated by (Sir) Richard Claverhouse Jebb (1841-1905), then Regius Professor of Greek in the University of Cambridge, whose own edition of Bacchylides was published in the year of his death.

UCLA Special Collections PA 3943.A2 1897.

52. Ulrich von Wilamowitz-Moellendorff, autograph letter to Sir Richard Jebb, acknowledging copy of the Bacchylides.

UCLA Special Collections Ms. 100 box 67 folder III.

53. *Der Timotheos Papyrus gefunden bei Abusir am 1. February 1902* [herausgegeben von Ulrich von Wilamowitz-Moellendorff], Leipzig: J. C. Hinrichs'sche Buchhandlung, 1903. **One of the earliest Greek manuscripts to survive. It is assigned to s. IV B.C.E. and was found with the skeleton of its owner.

UCLA URL *PJ 3721 B12K83.

54. *Lyra Graeca* translated by J. M. Edmonds, 1940 (Cambridge: Harvard University Press / London: William Heinemann Ltd, 1945) (Loeb Classical Library). **Translation of Timotheus.

UCLA URL PA 3611 A15 1928 v. 3 c. 2.

55. (Sir) F. G. Kenyon, "Recent Greek Literary Discoveries" *Classical Review* vol. VII no. 9, November 1893, pp. 429-431. **In the Archduke Rainer's Collection, in Vienna, a wooden board was recognised to include texts copied by a schoolboy from Euripides's *Phoenissae* and Callimachus's *Hecale*. "Nail-marks in the wood show that the board was originally suspended by a cord, so that either side could be brought to view; and there can be no doubt that it was intended for educational purposes". The board itself measured 1 foot 8 1/2 inches long by 3 1/4 to 4 inches in height.

> UCLA URL PA 1 C58 v. 7.

56. Newspaper cutting of E. G. Turner, "Complete Comedy of Menander". **Announcement of the discovery of Menander's *Dyscolus*.

> Private Collection.

57. *Papyrus Bodmer IV: Ménandre: Le Dyscolos publié* par Victor Martin, Cologny-Geneva: Bibliotheca Bodmeriana, 1958. **The editio princeps of Menander's *Dyscolus* or "Bad Tempered Man". The present copy once belonged to the Oxford classical scholar Maurice Platnauer.

> Private Collection.

58. A *Service in Memory of Eric Gardner Turner 26 February 1911 - 20 April 1983, Honorary Fellow of University College London and Emeritus Professor of Papyrology in the University of London, Founder-Director Institute of Classical Studies*, [London 1983].

> Private Collection.

DOCUMENTARY PAPYRI

Wall Case III

59. *The Hibeh Papyri part I* edited with Translations and Notes by Bernard P. Grenfell and Arthur S. Hunt, London: Sold at the Offices of the Egypt Exploration Fund, 1906 (Egypt Exploration Fund, Graeco-Roman Branch). **The papyri of El Hibeh mostly date to the third century before the common era. They included literary texts, e.g. of Homer and Euripides, Lysias and Epicharmus. On display is a Calendar for the Saite Nome (301-240 B.C.E.) (P. Hib. 1.27).

> UCLA URL PA 3315 H52686 v. 1

60. *The Tebtunis Papyri part I* edited by Bernard P. Grenfell, Arthur S. Hunt, and J. Gilbart Smyly, London: Henry Frowde, 1902 (University of California Publications, Graeco-Roman Archaeology, Volume 1). **The discovery of these papyri was due to bad temper.

> The tombs of the large Ptolemaic necropolis adjoining the town proved in many instances to contain only crocodiles, and on Jan. 16, 1900 . . . one of our workman, disgusted at finding a row of crocodiles where he expected sarcophagi, broke one of them in pieces

24

and disclosed the surprising fact that the creature was wrapped in sheets of papyrus. As may be imagined, after this find we dug out all the crocodile-tombs in the cemetery; and in the next few weeks several thousands of these animals were unearthed, of which a small portion (about 2 per cent.) contained papyri.

One of these papyri proved to be "A copy of a letter to Asclepiades, superintendant of revenues, . . . probably from a high official at Alexandria, . . . to Horus the basilico-gram mateus, announcing the approaching visit to the Fayûm of a Roman senator, Lucius Memmius, and giving directions for his reception and entertainment" (P. Tebt. 33: 112 B.C.E.).

UCLA URL DE 3 C12 v. 1.

61. *Papyri from Karanis: Third Series (Michigan Papyri, Vol. IX)* edited by Elinor M. Husselman, Published for the American Philological Association by the Press of Case Western Reserve University, 1971. **P. Kar. 562, 571, plates X-XI. On the left, the papyrus represents a lease of grain land and olive groves (119 C.E.); on the right, the papyrus includes two documents, the upper cancelled by cross-hatching (96) acknowledged receipt of a deposit of 740 drachmas from Lucius Iulius Celer by Gaius Iulius Sabinus, both soldiers in the Legio III Cyrenaica; the lower, a receipt of Gaius Iulius Clemens of Legio XXII for 580 drachmas from the original 740 drachmas (ca 98).

UCLA URL P 11 A51p no. 29.

62. *The Oxyrhynchus Papyri part I: edited with Translations and Notes by Bernard P. Grenfell and Arthur S. Hunt,* London: Sold at The Offices of the Egypt Exploration Fund, 1898. **Letter from the young Theon threatening never to speak to his father again unless he is taken with him to Alexandria (P. Oxy. 1.119: s. II or III).

UCLA URL *PA 3315 O9 v. 1.

63. Tony Reekmans, *A Sixth Century Account of Hay (P. Iand. inv. 653)*, Bruxelles: Fondation Égyptologique reine Élisabeth, 1962.

UCLA SRLF A 000 098 232 2.

THE RECOVERY OF CLASSICAL MANUSCRIPTS
IN THE RENASCENCE AND THE NINETEENTH CENTURY

Wall Case IV

64. [*ΙΛΙΑΣ ΟΜΗΡΟΥ Ilias Homeri*, Florence: Bartolomeo di Libri per Bernard e Neri Nerli, 1488.] **The editio princeps of Homer's *Iliad*. No writer is better represented in extant papyri than Homer. Until the 19th century, the earliest extant manuscripts were not older than the tenth century: fragments from the third century B.C.E. survive in papyri.

> UCLA Special Collections *A 1 H75p v. 1.

65. *ΘΟΥΚΥΔΙΔΗΣ. Thucydides*, Venetiis: in domo Aldi, May 1502. **The editio princeps of Thucydides's *History of the Peloponnesian War*. The earliest extant manuscript dates to the tenth century; the earliest papyrus fragment, probably from the third century B.C.E.

> UCLA Special Collections * Z 233 A4T42 c. 2.

66. *ΑΠΑΝΤΑ ΤΑ ΤΟΥ ΠΛΑΤΩΝΟΣ. Omnia Platonis opera*, Venetiis: in aedibus Aldi et Andreae soceri, Sept. 1513. **The editio princeps of Plato. In manuscript, Plato's oldest representative dates to 895 C.E.: in papyrus, to the third century B.C.E.

> UCLA Special Collections *Z 233 A4P69 v. 1-2. From the library of Thomas
> More's son-in-law, John Clement.

67. *Eusebii Pamphili Caesariensis episcopi Chronicon bipartitum nunc primum ex Armeniaco textu in Latinum conversum adnotationibus auctum Graecis fragmentis exornatum* opera P. Jo: Baptistae Aucher Ancyrani, Monachi Armeni et doctoris Mechitaristae, Venetiis: typis coenobii pp. Armenorum in insula S. Lazari, 1818. **Until this edition, Eusebius's *Chronicle* was known only from excerpts and from a Latin translation of one book.

> UCLA Special Collections D 17 E91c 1818 (K. M. Khantamour
> Armenian Collection).

68. *M. Cornelii Frontonis opera inedita cum epistulis item ineditis Antonini Pii, M. Aurelii, L. Veri et Appiani nec non aliorum veterum fragmentis* invenit et commentario praevio notisque illustravit Angelus Maius, Pars prior, Mediolani: regiis typis, 1815. **The first edition of Fronto's lost letters.

> Private Collection.

69. *M. Tulli Ciceronis de re publica quae supersunt* edente Angelo Maio, Stuttgartiae et Tubingae: in libraria Cottae, 1822. **One of the works which scholars hoped would be found among the Herculanean papyri, Cicero's Republic survives only in a palimpsest discovered by Angelo Mai. (In papyri, however, fragments of several of Cicero's writings have been found in Egypt; at Herculaneum, thus far, Latin texts have been few, notably fragments assigned to Ennius and Lucretius.)

UCLA URL PA 6296 D8 1822.

70. *Catullus. Carmina. Codex Oxoniensis: bibliothecae Bodleianae canonicanus class. Lat. 30* praefatus est R. A. B. Mynors, Lugduni Batavorum: A. W. Sijthoff, 1966. **No papyri of Catullus have yet been discovered, though a fragment of Cornelius Gallus was identified in the 1970s.

UCLA URL **PA 6274 A21375a.

Printed in Great Britain
by Amazon

41413232R10030